Tip it in!

Written by Alexandra Wells

Illustrated by Parwinder Singh

Collins

Sit in it.

Nat sits in it.

Tip pads in.

Nat tips pads in.

Nat taps a pan.

Tip pans in.

A map. A tin.

Tip tins in!

Dad taps it in.

Tap tap it in.

Sip it. Sip it.

Tap tap it in.

/n/

After reading

Letters and Sounds: Phase 2

Word count: 44

Focus phonemes: /s/ /a/ /t/ /p/ /i/ /n/ /m/ /d/

Curriculum links: Understanding the World; PSHE

Early learning goals: Reading: read and understand simple sentences; use phonic knowledge to decode regular words and read them aloud accurately; demonstrate understanding when talking with others about what they have read

Developing fluency

- Your child may enjoy hearing you read the book.
- You could take turns to read a page, with your child reading all the left-hand pages and you reading all the right-hand pages.

Phonic practice

- Turn to page 3. Ask your child to find a word containing the /a/ sound. (*Nat*)
- Ask them to sound out and blend the word.
- Turn to pages 8 and 9. Ask your child to find all the words containing the /i/ sound. (*tip, tins, in*)
- Ask them to sound out and blend each word. (t/i/p/ – **tip**; t/i/n/s – **tins**; i/n – **in**)
- Look at the "I spy sounds" pages (14–15). Ask your child to find items in the image that contain the /n/ sound. (e.g. *nuts, sandwiches, noodles, newspapers, melons, pans, necklaces*)

Extending vocabulary

- Pretend to be Nat in the shop, and make up a sentence beginning: "I tip in …" (e.g. *I tip in a can.; I tip in a packet of crisps.*)
- Pretend to be the girl on page 13, and make up a sentence beginning: "I tap in …" (e.g. *I tap in a can of beans.; I tap in a box of biscuits.*)